I0238143

The New 'Parents' Time Off' Series

# KIDS' HANDS-ON CRAFT ACTIVITIES

Linda Swainger

*Illustrations by*
Peter Petrovic

*Edited by*
Cecilia Egan

First published in 1995 by Pancake Press
as Kids' Craft Activities
Revised and updated 2015
Copyright © Leaves of Gold Press 2015

All rights reserved. No part of this book may be reproduced or transmitted by any person or entity (including Google, Amazon or similar organisations) in any form or by any means, electronic or mechanical, including photocopying, recording or by any information storage and retrieval system, without prior permission in writing from the publisher.

National Library of Australia Cataloguing-in-Publication entry
Creator: Swainger, Linda, author.
Title: Kids' hands-on craft activities / Linda Swainger ;
Peter Petrovic, illustrator.
Cecilia Egan, editor.

Edition: 2nd edition
ISBN: 9781925110715 (paperback)
Series: Parents' time off series ; 4.
Target Audience: For primary school age (6-12 year old)

Subjects: Handicraft for children.
Handicraft--Juvenile literature.
Creative activities and seat work.

Other Creators/Contributors:
Petrovic, Peter, illustrator.

Dewey Number: 745.5083

ABN 67 099 575 078
PO Box 9113, Brighton, 3186, Victoria, Australia
www.leavesofgoldpress.com

# CONTENTS

Mobiles ............................................................. 1
Dressing Up ..................................................... 11
Headpieces ...................................................... 17
Puppets ........................................................... 23
Christmas Decorations ................................... 29
Gift Wrapping Papers ..................................... 37
Making Musical Instruments ......................... 43
Make Your Own Puzzles ................................ 49
Useful Containers ........................................... 53
Paper and Card Craft .................................... 59
Obtaining Materials ....................................... 65
Index ............................................................... 69

## INTRODUCTION

Author Linda Swainger is a teacher with a flair for craft and a love of children. Of all the craft activities she has come to know through trial and experience, she has chosen these because they are the most rewarding for children and the easiest to do at home.

The activities have a wide range. They can be done by the very young and also by older children who can make the more complicated variations.

Illustrations are simple and easy to copy.

Children will love the colourful and varied projects in this delightful book.

# MOBILES

Bird Mobile
Spiral Mobile
Cork Mobile
Felt Animal Mobile

# BIRD MOBILE

**Materials:**
- Three sticks the same size
- String
- Scissors
- Heavy card
- Hole punch
- Brightly coloured pencils, paints or felt tip pens

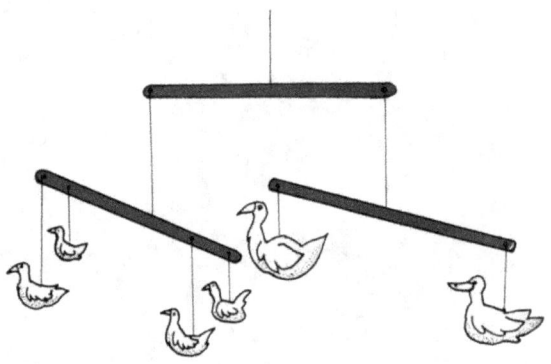

**Instructions:**
1. Draw four birds on the piece of card.
2. Cut out the birds and paint them brightly on both sides.
3. Punch a hole in each bird and attach the string to them. The string on each bird should be the same length.
4. Construct the mobile as seen above. Adjust the balance by moving the strings along the stick.

**Variations:**
- Make an animal mobile or use a theme, i.e. farms or families.
- If you want to have parents and babies as pictured make the smaller figures approximately half the size of the others and have two babies for each adult for balance.

# SPIRAL MOBILE

**Materials:**
- Large round plate
- Pencil
- Paints, bright crayon or pencils
- String
- Heavy card
- Hole punch
- Various bright bits and pieces for hanging, e.g. corks, bottle tops, buttons, tin foil bits.

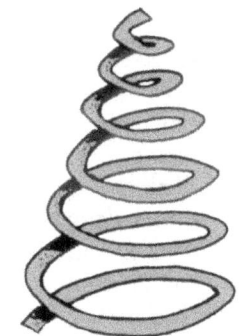

**Instructions:**
1. Using the card and pencil, trace around the paper plate.
2. Cut out the circle and paint the card using a different colour for each side.
3. When dry, draw a spiral as shown above onto the card, leaving a small circle in the middle.
4. Cut along the spiral lines.
5. Attach a piece of string to the small (middle) circle and hang various bright objects at different intervals down the spiral.

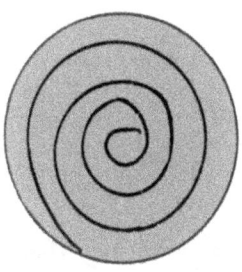

**Variation:**
- Instead of 'bits and pieces' hang smaller spirals at different intervals.

# CORK MOBILE

**Materials:**
- *Sewing pins*
- *Corks*
- *String*
- *Three sticks - similar length*
- *Pipe cleaners, coloured card, felt*
- *Strong glue*

**Instructions - Master Method**
1. Using the corks and bits and pieces make a variety of animals or objects for your mobile, i.e. spiders, birds, bees, butterflies, etc. See below.
2. Attach a piece of string to each cork object using a pin.
3. Construct the mobile as seen above. Adjust the balance by moving the string along the sticks.

**Variation:**
- Make the mobile as above using cotton reels instead of corks.

# CORK MOBILE (Continued)

## CORK BEES

**Materials:**
- Three black pipe cleaners eight cm long
- Yellow and black paper
- Glad Wrap or other plastic food wrap
- Scissors
- Five sewing pins
- Glue
- One black pipe cleaner three cm long
- One small elastic band

**Instructions:**
1. Attach the legs by folding each 8 centimeter long pipe cleaner in half and around a pin. Insert in a line on the cork. This will form the underside leg section.
2. Attach the feelers by folding the 3 centimeter long pipe cleaner around a pin (in the same manner as 1.) and inserting into one end of the cork.
3. Cut the yellow and black paper into thin strips and glue to the upperside of the bee - this will form the back section.
4. Construct the wings by folding in half an 8 cm by 10 cm piece of Glad Wrap. Fold the longest side so it becomes 5 centimeters wide.
5. Scrunch the centre part of the wings together and hold this in place with an elastic band. Attach this to the bee's back using a pin through the centre elastic band section. Shape the wings with the scissors if desired.

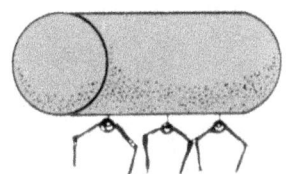
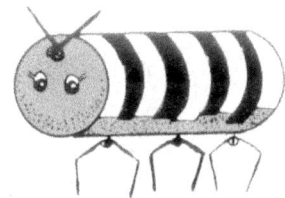

# CORK MOBILE (Continued)

### CORK BUTTERFLIES
- Use the bee method to make the butterfly, but omit the yellow and black stripes and add either paint dots or coloured paper dots (i.e. confetti) glued to the wings.

You can also make the wings slightly larger.

### CORK SPIDERS
- Use the bee method omitting stripes and wings. Paint the body section black.

### CORK BIRDS

**Materials:**
- *Strong card (desired colour)*
- *Scissors*
- *Sewing pins*
- *Pencil*

**Instructions:**
1. Draw and cut out two wing sections using the shape above as a guide.
2. Fold each wing section along the dotted line and attach to each side of the cork using sewing pins through the folded piece of card.

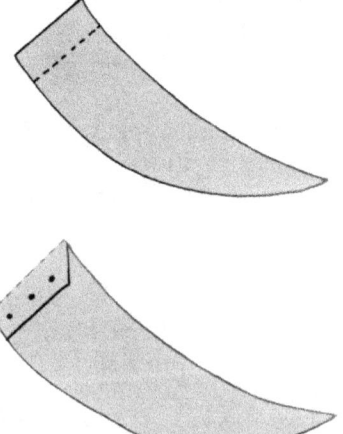

# FELT ANIMAL MOBILE (Continued)

## Felt Giraffe
The giraffe's neck can be stiffened by cutting two felt body shapes and a cardboard shape, and gluing the cardboard in between.

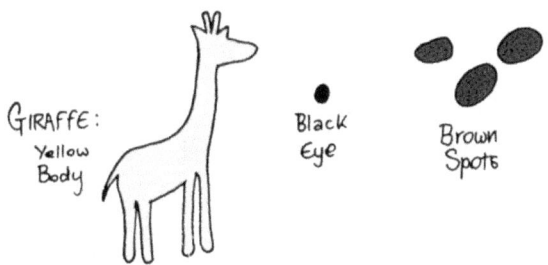

## Felt Dog

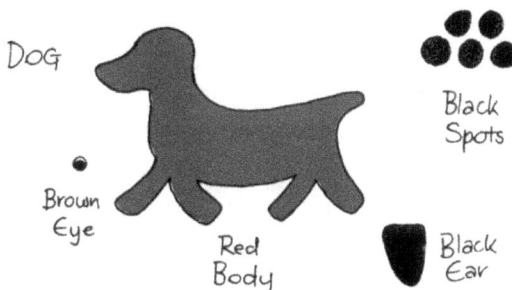

## Variations:
- Make the above mobile but use a theme, e.g. Christmas, Australian Animals, the Farm.

# DRESSING UP

Space Creature
Cat Dress-Up
Doctor Dress-Up
Sandwich Advertising Board
Other Ideas for Dressing Up

# SPACE CREATURE

**Materials:**
- *Four cardboard egg cartons*
- *Cardboard box approximately 20 cm x 20 cm x 20 cm.*
- *Strong glue*
- *Shorts or short skirt*
- *Shirt with buttons*
- *Paint*

**Instructions:**
1. Cut away one side of the cardboard box so that it fits over the head.
2. Open out the egg cartons and using the cup sections paste one each onto three sides of the box and one on the top.
3. Cut out square holes for eyes and a rectangle for the mouth.
4. Paint the 'space head' whatever colour you like. Preferably to match the colour of clothes you will be wearing.
5. Now put your shorts on. Put your shirt on back to front so that the buttons are at the back.
6. Put on your 'Space Head' and you're ready.

# FELT ANIMAL MOBILE (Continued)

### Felt Giraffe
The giraffe's neck can be stiffened by cutting two felt body shapes and a cardboard shape, and gluing the cardboard in between.

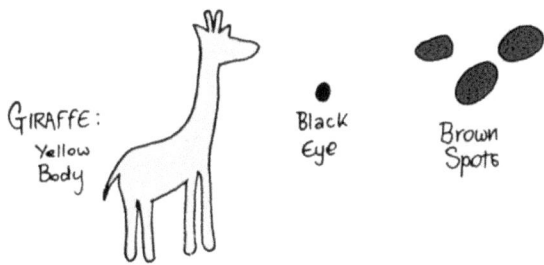

### Felt Dog

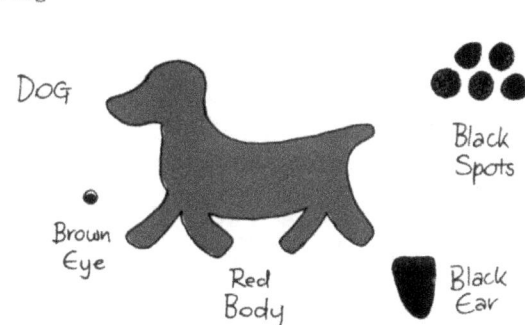

### Variations:
- Make the above mobile but use a theme, e.g. Christmas, Australian Animals, the Farm.

# CAT DRESS-UP

**Materials:**
- *Circle of elastic to fit around the face*
- *Circle of elastic to fit around the waist.*
- *Old stockings*
- *Newspaper*
- *Heavy card*
- *Needle and thread*
- *Scissors*
- *Black eye liner or face paint*
- *Paint or felt pens*

**Instructions:**
1. Using the heavy card draw two triangular ears. Cut these out and colour them the appropriate colour for your cat.
2. Sew the triangular ears onto the piece of face elastic.
3. Cut one of the stocking legs off. This will form the tail.
4. Roll the newspaper into small balls and stuff it into the stocking leg firmly.
5. Sew the top of the stocking leg onto the elastic waist band.
6. Put on your ears and tail and paint some whiskers on your face.

## DOCTOR DRESS-UP

**Materials:**
- Large white shirt
- Thick white elastic to fit around the head
- Heavy card
- Scissors
- Tinfoil
- Strong glue
- Needle and thread

**Instructions:**
1. Sew the elastic's ends together so that it fits snugly around your head.
2. Draw a circle onto the card approximately 3.5 cm in diameter and cut this out.
3. Apply glue to both sides of this circle and cover it with tinfoil.
4. Using the needle and thread sew the tinfoil circle to the elastic circle.
5. Put on the white shirt and the headpiece and you're ready.

## SANDWICH ADVERTISING BOARD

**Materials:**
- *Two large pieces of heavy card big enough to cover the body almost to the knees.*
- *Four pieces of thick elastic 15 cm long*
- *Needle and thread*
- *Paints*

**Instructions:**
1. Join the two pieces of card using the elastic, needle and thread. Ensure that the placement of the elastic allows it to sit comfortably on your shoulders.
2. Now join the sides of the heavy card in the same way.
3. Now decorate the card with something on it, e.g. "Vegemite" or just paint a nice picture on the front and back.

**Note:** You may find it easier to punch holes in the card with skewer or knitting needle.

## OTHER IDEAS FOR DRESSING UP

- **Elephants:** - using a stocking for the trunk, cardboard shapes on elastic headband for ears.
- **Clowns:** - painted faces and fabric lengths around neck, ankles and wrists.
- **Magicians:** - make a cardboard hat with foil stars glued on and use a towel for a cape.
- **Scarecrow:** - put on large old clothes and a hat and stuff straw into the collars and cuffs. Paint on a funny face with makeup.

# HEADPIECES

Indian Girl Headpiece
Spaceman
Swagman
Witch
Princess Headpiece
Spider

# INDIAN GIRL HEADPIECE

**Materials:**
- Length of elastic to fit around head
- Needle and thread
- Scissors
- Lengths of wool 60cm long (6 bundles of 15 strands)
- Extra wool

**Instructions:**
1. Using the needle and thread sew the two ends of the elastic together to make a circle that fits around your head.
2. Gather together a bundle of wool strands (i.e. about 45 strands)
3. Fold the wool in half and hang it over one part of the elastic circle. Fasten with wool.

Example

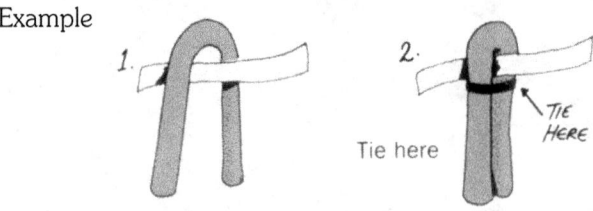

4. Divide the bundle into 3 equal parts and plait the wool.
5. Finish the plait approximately 2 cm from the end of the wool and wrap some of the extra wool around the end and tie.
6. Plait the other side the same way using steps 2,3,4 and 5.

Now your Indian Girl Headpiece is ready.

**Variations:**
For an Indian Boy Headpiece, make a headband from a cardboardstrip and tape on a real or drawn feather.

# SPACEMAN

**Materials:**
- Sharp scissors
- Icecream container
- Silver paint pen
- Two pipe cleaners
- Two pom poms or cotton wool balls
- Sticky tape and strong paste

**Instructions:**
1. Using the scissors pierce two holes in the top of the icecream container.
2. Put the end of one pipe cleaner through each hole and secure with sticky tape.

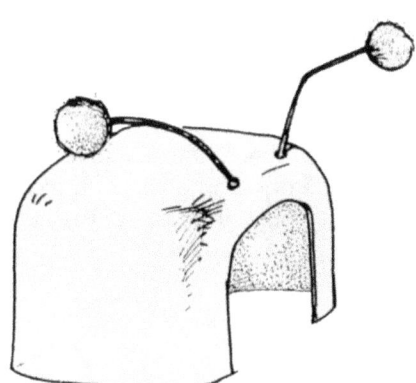

3. Using the strong paste attach a pom pom to the end of each pipe cleaner.
4. Cut away a section of one of the sides of the ice cream container. This will be the face section.

Example

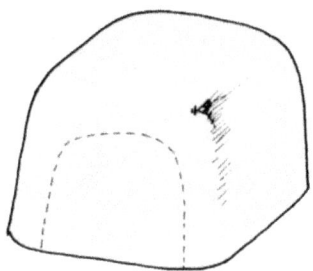

5. Decorate the space hat with the silver paint pen.

## SWAGMAN

**Materials:**
- Cloth wide-brimmed hat
- Corks
- Needle and thread
- Sewing pins

**Instructions:**
1. Cut the thread into 10cm lengths. As many as you have corks.
2. Tie a knot in one end of a piece of string, thread it onto the needle and through the cloth of the hat brim.

Example

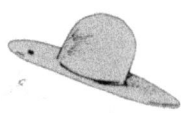 

3. Tie the other end of the piece of string around a pin head and insert it into a cork.
4. Repeat steps 2 and 3 right around the hat.

## WITCH

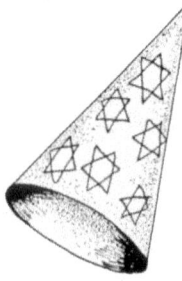 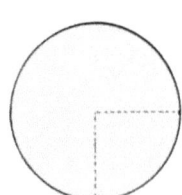

**Materials:**
- Cardboard
- Tinfoil
- Scissors
- Strong paste
- Black paper

**Instructions:**
1. Cut a circle 60 cm in diameter.
2. Now cut a quarter out of the circle.
3. Join the remaining three quarters of the circle together with the paste.
4. Put plenty of paste on the hat and cover it with black paper.
5. Using the remaining foil cut out different sized stars.
6. Paste them onto the hat.

## PRINCESS HEADPIECE

**Materials:**
- Cardboard
- Paints or tinfoil
- Scissors
- Paste

**Instructions:**
1. Cut a strip of cardboard about 3cm in thickness and long enough to go around your head.
2. Paste the ends together to form a circle.
3. Draw a crown on the remaining card and cut it out.

   Example

4. Attach the crown to the headband and paint the whole lot **or** wrap it with tinfoil.

## SPIDER

**Materials:**
- Six black pipe cleaners
- Strip of thin card or elastic
- Sticky tape
- Textas or other felt pens

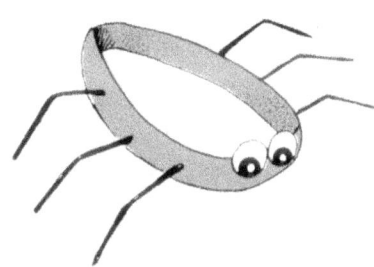

**Instructions:**
1. Cut the card or elastic to fit snugly around the head - tape the two ends together to form a circle.
2. Attach the pipe cleaners with tape and form the legs.
3. Make some eyes with the felt pens and extra card and glue them on.

# PUPPETS

Materials for Puppet-Making
Felt Finger Puppets
Cardboard Finger Puppets
Paper Plate Puppets
Rubber Glove Puppets
Toilet Roll Puppets

# MATERIALS FOR PUPPET-MAKING

**Waste Materials which can be used for Puppet Making**
- Streamers
- Staples
- Cardboard cylinders
- Paper plates
- Cotton wool
- Cardboard cones
- Wool
- Fabric scraps
- Fur pieces
- Pipe cleaners
- Stickers
- Ribbon
- Feathers
- Foil
- Toilet rolls
- Yoghurt containers
- Small boxes
- Paper bags
- Socks
- Felt
- Paper cups
- Wrapping paper
- Coloured paper scraps

# FELT FINGER PUPPETS

**Materials:**
- Wooden clothes peg (any type)
- Needle and thread
- Small pieces of coloured felt or fabric
- Strong glue.
- Thin brush
- Two pieces of felt or strong fabric long enough and wide enough to fit over your finger.

**Instructions:**
1. Cut a piece of felt 10cm x 4cm. Fold this over and sew up each side.

   Example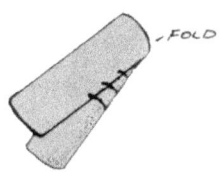

2. Now cut other coloured felt bits into appropriate pieces to make the puppet you like, e.g. pieces for a face hat etc as seen above.
3. Stick the pieces onto your puppet with the strong paste and sit the puppet over a clothes peg to dry (this makes sure it doesn't stick together).

**Variations:**
- Make the puppet as above but using heavy fabric such as corduroy or denim.
- Make a finger puppet family or story characters.

 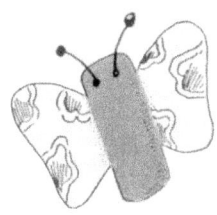

# CARDBOARD FINGER PUPPETS

**Materials:**
- *Card*
- *Scissors*
- *Pencils or felt tip pens*
- *Fabric scraps*
- *Strong glue*

**Instructions:**
1. Draw a figure 8 on a piece of card leaving a gap between the joining of the two circles.

   Example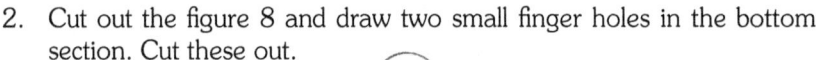

2. Cut out the figure 8 and draw two small finger holes in the bottom section. Cut these out.

   Example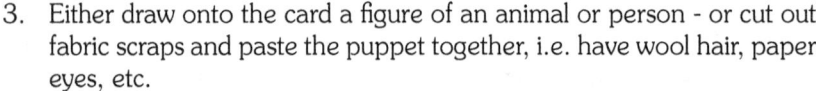

3. Either draw onto the card a figure of an animal or person - or cut out fabric scraps and paste the puppet together, i.e. have wool hair, paper eyes, etc.

**Variations:**
- Try to make the above puppets using different base shapes.

Example

# PAPER PLATE PUPPETS

**Materials:**
- *Paper plates*
- *Cardboard cylinders or sticks*
- *Strong glue*
- *Staples*
- *Waste materials*
- *Sticky tape*

**Instructions:**
1. Using the sticky tape attach the cardboard cylinder (or stick) to the front of the paper plate (This becomes the back of the puppet).
2. Using the waste materials and glue or staples construct your puppet adding hair, facial features, etc., as appropriate.
3. To cover your hand when it holds the puppet you can wrap some fabric around the cardboard cylinder.

**Suggestions**
Hair - wool, string, cotton wool, fur pieces.
Eyes - buttons, foil circles, drawn with felt tipped pens.
Nose - cork, buttons, drawn on.
Mouth - streamer, coloured paper, ribbon

**Variations:**
- Try making some animal puppets such as lions, elephants or ducks

- Try using paper plates of various sizes and shapes.

## RUBBER GLOVE PUPPETS

**Materials:**
- *Small rubber glove*
- *Felt tipped pens or Textas*

**Instructions:**
1. Put on the rubber glove and using the pens draw a character on each finger.

**Variations:**
- As above but stick waste materials onto each finger using strong glue to make people or animal type puppets, i.e. fabric clothes or wool hair.

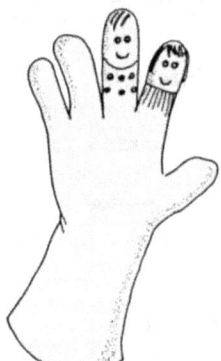

## TOILET ROLL PUPPETS

**Materials:**
- *Toilet roll cylinder*
- *Strong glue*
- *Waste materials for decoration*
- *Textas or felt-tipped pens.*

**Instructions:**
1. Use the waste materials to decorate the toilet roll. Add things like hats, hair, facial features, bold ties, fabric clothes hanging from the bottom. Use your imagination to create an amusing character.

# CHRISTMAS DECORATIONS

Cardboard Cone Christmas Trees
Magic Strips
Pasta Wreaths
Egg Cup Bells
Various Hanging Decorations
Dough Decorations

# CARDBOARD CONE CHRISTMAS TREES

**Materials:**
- *Cardboard cone (available from clothing manufacturers)*
- *Green crepe paper*
- *Stickers - stars/circles*
- *Brightly coloured paint*
- *Strong glue*

**Instructions:**
1. From the wad of crepe paper cut off a strip about 2.5 cm thick. Fringe one side of this.

Example

2. Unwrap the strip and paste it around the cardboard cone starting from the top. Make sure you don't stick the fringed edge down.
3. Decorate the Christmas Tree with the stickers or bright paint dollops.
4. Make a cardboard star and cover it with tinfoil for the top.

**Variations:**
- If you don't have a cardboard cone, cut a large circle from heavy card. Cut away a quarter of the circle and join the remaining three quarters.

  Example

  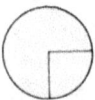

- Cover the cone with bright Christmas wrap instead of crepe paper.
- Decorate with cut out Santas, bells, etc. from Christmas wrap.

## MAGIC STRIPS

**Materials:**
- *Clear cellophane*
- *Small bright pieces of paper, coloured patty pans (otherwise known as paper cupcake holders), short strips of streamers, coloured rice (see "obtaining materials"), coloured sprinkles, glitter and any other bright, small objects.*
- *String or ribbon*
- *Strong glue*
- *Stapler*

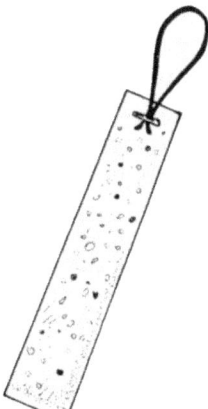

**Instructions:**
1. Cut cellophane into thin pieces of varying lengths for hanging, i.e. 20 cm.
2. Using the stapler carefully staple a loop of string or ribbon to one end of each cellophane piece to form the hanger.
3. Apply small spots of strong glue intermittently over the cellophane strips and put on the bright bits and pieces.
- When it's finished and hung on the tree it looks as if the bits and pieces are hanging in mid-air.

**Optional** - a spray of varnish over finished product

**Variation:**
- Try curling the cellophane strip with one edge of scissors prior to decorating.
- Instead of pasting on bits and pieces use paint spots either with a small brush or flicked on with a toothbrush.

## PASTA WREATHS

**Materials:**
- One paper plate
- Strong glue
- Assorted pasta - shells, spirals, macaroni, rice, dried peas, etc.
- Gold or silver spray paint
- Scissors, stapler
- Fishing line or coloured ribbon

**Instructions:**
1. Using the scissors carefully cut out the centre of the paper plate. Leaving it like a doughnut ring.

    Example

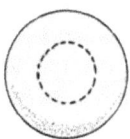

2. Using the fishing line, string or ribbon, staple a hanging loop to the plate.
3. Using lots of strong glue paste the pasta around the ring. The more that's on it the better the finished product looks.
4. When dry spray the wreath with the gold or silver spray paint.

# EGG CUP BELLS

**Materials:**
- Gold or silver paper, aluminium foil or Christmas wrap
- String
- Needle
- Scissors
- Egg carton cups
- Paste

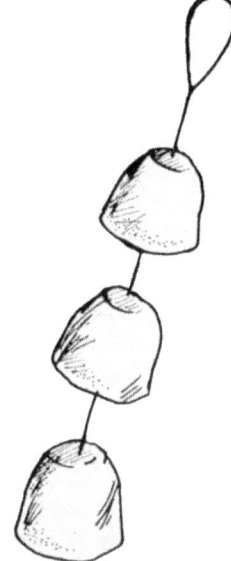

**Instructions:**
1. Using the coloured paper and paste wrap each egg carton cup tucking the ends up inside.
2. Using needle and string, thread each cup onto the string knotting it intermittently to separate the egg cups.

**Variations:**
- Paste glitter to the outside of wrapped cups.
- Hang each egg cup separately as an individual tree decoration.

## VARIOUS HANGING DECORATIONS

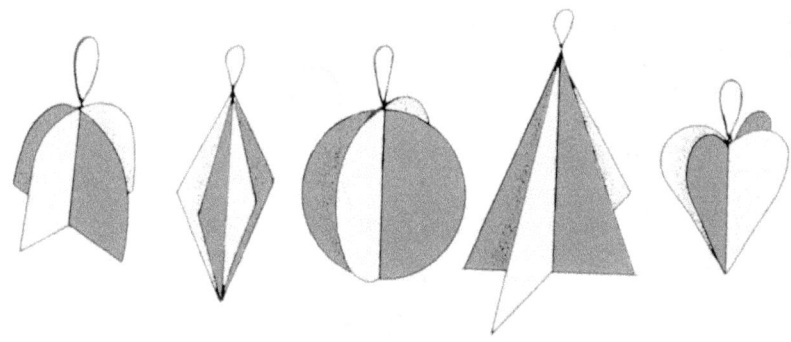

- Diamonds, bells, circles, stars, hearts, squares, etc., etc. can all be made using the following recipe.
1. Using light cardboard cut out two shapes of the same object, e.g. bells.
2. Make a cut half way up the middle of each, starting from opposite ends.

3. Join by sliding the two pieces together at the cut edges.
4. Decorate with glitter, foil or coloured paper.
5. Attach a string, fishing line or ribbon loop to hang from the tree.

# DOUGH DECORATIONS

**Dough**
2 cups plain flour
1 cup salt
enough water to form dough.

**Materials:**
- 1 quantity dough
- Christmas cookie cutters
- Oven tray
- Macaroni
- Rolling pin
- Varnish

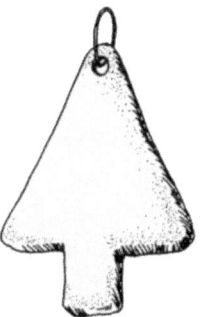

**Instructions:**
1. Make the dough by mixing sifted flour and salt with water until it mixes into a firm dough.
2. Knead the dough until it is soft and pliable then roll out to approximately 1 cm thickness.
3. Using the Christmas cutters cut out as many shapes as you can. Then re-roll the remaining dough and cut again. Place on oven tray cook and insert macaroni in the top to form a hole - leave while cooking.
4. Cook in a cool oven - 100°C (200°F) until dough is hard all over. Test by pressing at the thickest part. If there is any give continue to cook. (Be careful it doesn't burn).
5. When cooked and cooled remove the macaroni and insert fishing line to make a loop for hanging. Coat with 2 - 3 coats of varnish.

**Variations:**
- Sprinkle with glitter or decorate with paint before varnishing.
- If cutters are unavailable cut out your own shapes with a knife.

# GIFT WRAPPING PAPERS

String and Woodblock Print Wrap
Surprise Picture Wrap
Fan Fold Wrap
Vegetable Print Wrap
Clay Print Wrap

# STRING AND WOODBLOCK PRINT WRAP

**Materials:**
- *Two blocks of wood approximately 10cm x 5cm (or similar size)*
- *String or wool*
- *Paints and paint brush*
- *Sheets of paper, e.g. butcher's, computer or coloured tissue paper.*

**Instructions:**
1. Wrap the string around one of the woodblocks and tie the ends.

Example

2. Wrap and tie string on the second woodblock in a different way, i.e. closer together, further apart, criss crossing, etc.
3. Paint one side of each of the woodblocks and print with them on the large sheets of paper in an abstract way.

**Variation:**
- If wood blocks are unavailable, try wrapping the string around a box or cardboard roll for printing.

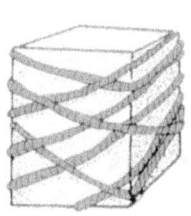

# SURPRISE PICTURE WRAP

**Materials:**
- *Eye droppers*
- *Paint*
- *Sheets of paper, e.g. computer, butcher's, or coloured tissue wrap.*

**Instructions:**
1. Fold the paper in half.
2. Dip an eyedropper into the paint and drop some drops on one half of the page only.
3. Repeat step 2 using different colours and making drops intermittently on one side of the page.
4. Fold the paper in half again smoothing it down with the palm of your hand. (This process spreads the paint around).
5. Open out the page and allow to dry.

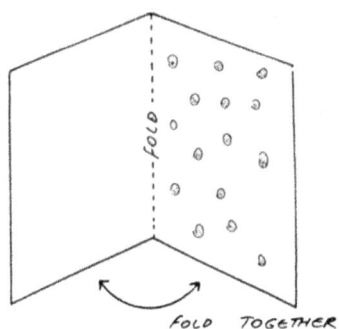

**Variation B**
- Instead of drops make short 'dribble' lines with the paint and eyedroppers.
- If eyedroppers are unavailable use a paint brush and thick paint.

## FAN FOLD WRAP

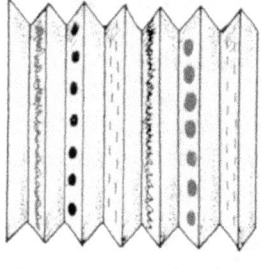

**Materials:**
- *Paper, i.e. computer or butcher's paper*
- *Paints*
- *Thin paint brushes or eye droppers*

**Instructions:**
1. Fold the paper in concertina (fan like) fashion.
2. Open out the paper and press flat.
3. Paint on every second section as seen in the picture above. Try to make each section different and be careful not to use too much paint.
4. Carefully re-fold in concertina fashion and gently press down to spread the paint.
5. Open out again and allow to dry.

## VEGETABLE PRINT WRAP

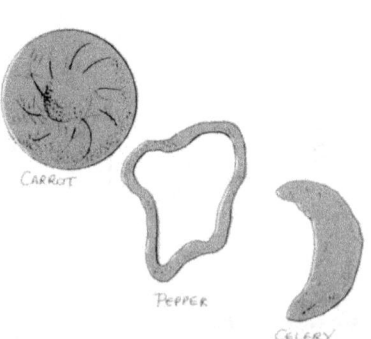

**Materials:**
- Assorted vegetables, i.e. carrot, celery, green pepper
- Paints and brushes
- Knife
- Paper, i.e. butcher's or computer paper

**Instructions:**
1. Cut across a piece of the vegetable into a size manageable in your hand.
2. Paint the cut surface with plenty of paint.
3. Print on the paper, covering as much as possible.

## CLAY PRINT WRAP

**Materials:**
- *Talcum powder*
- *Modelling clay, firm plasticine or dough*
- *Paint brush*
- *Pencil*
- *Paper - computer, butcher's or tissue paper*
- *Dough roller*

**Instructions:**
1. Roll the modelling material out flat.
2. Use the pencil to draw a picture on the flat surface of the modelling material.
3. Dust over the picture lightly with some powder then brush paint over the top of the powder.
4. Place the paper over the clay picture and gently rub over the top.
5. Wipe the paint off the clay with a damp cloth (not wet).
6. Repeat using the same picture or make different pictures to print over the paper.

# MAKING MUSICAL INSTRUMENTS

Tin Drum
Drumsticks
Light Globe Shaker
Shaker Filling
Basic Plastic Shaker
Lid Cymbals
Mellagerphone

# TIN DRUM

**Materials:**
- Strong glue and brush
- Wrapping paper
- One large tin, i.e. an empty coffee tin or extra large canned food tin or empty biscuit tin
- Scissors
- Clear self-adhesive book covering

**Instructions:**
1. Wash and dry the empty tin.
2. Cut your wrapping paper to the size of the outside of the tin. Example
3. Apply plenty of strong glue around the outside of the tin and attach the wrapping paper piece - press down firmly to ensure it all sticks.
4. Cut the self-adhesive book covering to the size of the outside of the tin (see Step 2).
5. When the wrapping paper and glue is dry cover the outside of the tin with the book covering.

**Variations:**
- Cover the tin with magazine picture cut outs.
- Cover the tin with lots of coloured shapes all overlapping.

## DRUMSTICKS

**Materials:**
- *Two pieces of 20 cm dowling*
- *Sandpaper*
- *Varnish*

**Instructions:**
- Use the sandpaper to remove any rough edges and apply two to three coats of varnish.

## LIGHT GLOBE SHAKER

**Materials:**
- *One old light globe*
- *Old newspaper*
- *Coloured or wrapping paper*
- *Glue*

**Instructions:**
1. Tear the newspaper into strips approximately 4 cm wide by 10 cm long.
2. Put the glue in a bowl, immerse one sheet of newspaper in it at a time. When it's wet cover the light globe with it.
3. When the globe is covered with three or four layers of newspaper paste the coloured or wrapping paper over the top of the newspaper. Allow several days to dry.
4. When the globe and paper is dry and hard, bang it sharply to break the glass inside. Now give it a shake.

## SHAKER FILLINGS

- Sand
- Stones
- Dirt
- Rice
- Macaroni
- Dried peas
- Dried soup mix
- Beans
- Pasta or a mixture of these
- A mixture of the above.

## BASIC PLASTIC SHAKER

**Materials:**
- *Container with lid, i.e. cream bottle, cordial bottle or empty tin, any size.*
- *Shaker filling, (see above.)*
- *Paper to decorate, i.e. coloured paper shapes and streamers*
- *Glue*
- *Spray varnish or clear, self-adhesive book covering.*

**Instructions:**
1. Wash and dry the plastic container.
2. Put approximately two to three tablespoons of shaker filling into the container and put the lid on.
3. Cut the coloured paper or wrapping paper into lots of shapes and paste these onto the container overlapping them so the entire container, including the lid, is covered.
4. When dry spray with two to three coats of varnish or cover with clear, self-adhesive book covering.

**Variations:**
- Staple together two decorated paper plates filled with shaker filling.

## LID CYMBALS

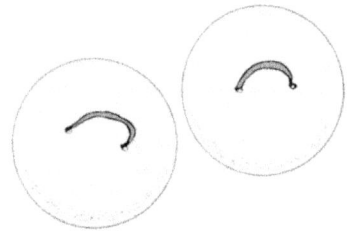

**Materials:**
- *String or ribbon*
- *Two metal lids, i.e. from coffee or biscuit tins*
- *Hammer and thick nail*

**Instructions:**
1. Using the hammer and nail carefully make two holes in each of the lids.
2. Use the ribbon or string and make a loop. Insert one end through one hole and back out the other. Tie.
3. Repeat Step 2 with the other lid and your cymbals are ready for use.

## MELLAGERPHONE

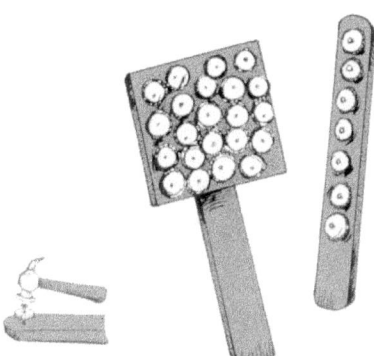

**Materials:**
- *Hammer*
- *Packet of 3 cm long nails*
- *Long piece of wood (Figure 2) or two pieces constructed as in Figure 1.*
- *Bottle tops - either from soft drinks or beer bottles*
- *Varnish or paint*

**Instructions:**
1. Varnish or paint the piece of wood as you like.
2. Carefully wash and dry the bottle tops ready for use.
3. When the wood piece is dry hammer nails through the bottle tops attaching them to the wood piece.

Note: Do not hammer the nails in too tightly; allow the bottle tops room to shake about.

# MAKE YOUR OWN PUZZLES

Make your Own Jigsaws
Double-sided Puzzles
Multi-sided Box Puzzles

# MAKE YOUR OWN JIGSAWS

**Materials:**
- *Thick card*
- *Paste*
- *Scissors*
- *Textas or paints*
- *Varnish*

**Instructions:**
1. Paint or draw a bright colourful picture onto a square piece of the card.
2. When the picture is completely dry varnish with two to three coats of varnish.
3. Now cut up the puzzle into interesting shapes. You might find it easier to use a pencil to draw puzzle pieces before cutting.

**Variation:**
- Instead of painting or drawing a picture, you could cut out a picture from a magazine, paste it onto the card and cut it up.
- You could also paste wrapping paper onto the card to make your puzzle.

How about making some hard puzzles for your friends?

# DOUBLE-SIDED PUZZLES

### Materials:
- *Nine empty match boxes*
- *Two pictures*
- *Paste*
- *Ruler*
- *Pencil*
- *Scissors*
- *Varnish*

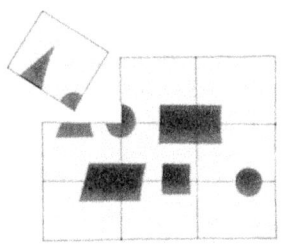

### Instructions:
1. Using the pencil and ruler draw rectangles on the rear of the picture the same size as the matchbox.
2. Cut along the lines with the scissors.
3. Paste each rectangular picture onto one side of each matchbox.
4. When this side of the puzzle is dry varnish it with two to three coats of varnish.
5. Making sure pieces are in the right places, turn over each matchbox
6. Repeat steps 1,2,3, and 4 with the second picture.

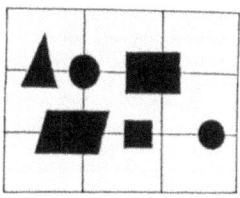

STEP 1

### Variation:
- Now use harder pictures, i.e. magazine pictures, or wrapping paper.

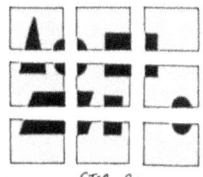

STEP 2

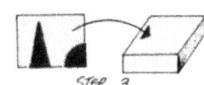

STEP 3

# MULTI-SIDED BOX PUZZLE

**Materials:**
- Nine boxes the same size (preferably cube shaped)
- Six pictures big enough to cover every side
- Paste
- Scissors
- Ruler
- Pencil
- Varnish

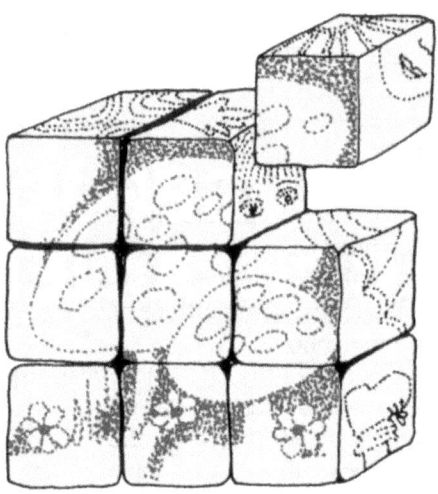

**Instructions:**
1. Place all the boxes together with the same sides facing.
2. Take one picture and using the pencil and ruler divide the picture into the same sized squares or rectangles as the boxes.
3. Cut along the lines with the scissors.
4. Paste each picture piece onto the same side of each box.
5. When the pictures are dry varnish with two to three coats of varnish.
6. When the varnish is dry make the puzzle so each piece is in the correct place and turn each box one turn to the left
7. Repeat steps 1,2,3,4,5 and 6 until all sides of the boxes have pictures on them.
8. Now mess up your puzzle and try to put it together again.

# USEFUL CONTAINERS

Design-it-Yourself Storage Boxes
Toy Bags
Desk Sets
Plant Pots
Notepad Holder

# DESIGN IT YOURSELF STORAGE BOXES

**Materials:**
- *Three large boxes the same size*
- *Bright paints*
- *Varnish*

**Instructions:**
1. Place the boxes either end to end in a line or one on top of the other to form a tall storage space.
2. Using bright paints, paint a picture right across (or down) all three boxes.
3. Repeat step 2 on the other three sides of the boxes.
4. Varnish each side of each box with two to three coats of varnish.
5. When they're dry you can use them to store toys or other objects. Turning them around like a puzzle makes 'misfit' pictures.

Example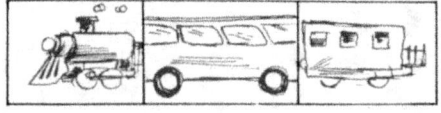

**Variations:**
- Use smaller boxes and store toys, dolls or odds and ends in them.
- Cover the boxes with wrapping paper.

# DOUBLE-SIDED PUZZLES

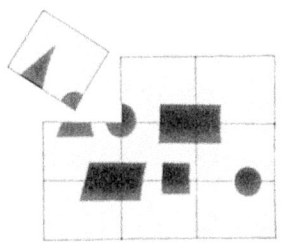

### Materials:
- *Nine empty match boxes*
- *Two pictures*
- *Paste*
- *Ruler*
- *Pencil*
- *Scissors*
- *Varnish*

### Instructions:
1. Using the pencil and ruler draw rectangles on the rear of the picture the same size as the matchbox.
2. Cut along the lines with the scissors.
3. Paste each rectangular picture onto one side of each matchbox.
4. When this side of the puzzle is dry varnish it with two to three coats of varnish.
5. Making sure pieces are in the right places, turn over each matchbox
6. Repeat steps 1,2,3, and 4 with the second picture.

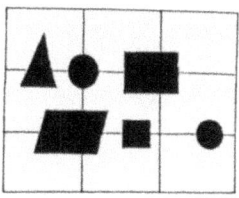

STEP 1

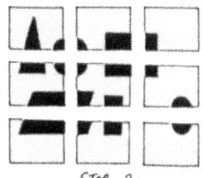

STEP 2

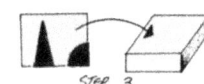

STEP 3

### Variation:
- Now use harder pictures, i.e. magazine pictures, or wrapping paper.

# MULTI-SIDED BOX PUZZLE

**Materials:**
- Nine boxes the same size (preferably cube shaped)
- Six pictures big enough to cover every side
- Paste
- Scissors
- Ruler
- Pencil
- Varnish

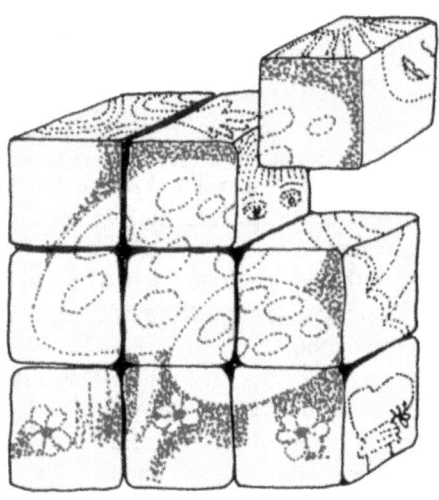

**Instructions:**
1. Place all the boxes together with the same sides facing.
2. Take one picture and using the pencil and ruler divide the picture into the same sized squares or rectangles as the boxes.
3. Cut along the lines with the scissors.
4. Paste each picture piece onto the same side of each box.
5. When the pictures are dry varnish with two to three coats of varnish.
6. When the varnish is dry make the puzzle so each piece is in the correct place and turn each box one turn to the left
7. Repeat steps 1,2,3,4,5 and 6 until all sides of the boxes have pictures on them.
8. Now mess up your puzzle and try to put it together again.

# TOY BAGS

**Materials:**
- *An old shirt*
- *Needle and thread (or ask mum to do this on the sewing machine*
- *fabric paints or crayons*
- *coat hanger*

**Instructions:**
1. Using the needle and thread sew the back and front of the shirt together at the bottom. If this is too hard ask an adult to help you.
2. Using the fabric paints, carefully noting their instructions, draw bright pictures on the front and back of the shirt.
3. Hang the shirt on the coat hanger and you have a good toy bag to hang in your room.

**Variations:**
- Do the same as above, but use a pillow case instead of a shirt. Put a hole in the inside lip of the case for the coat hanger.

# DESK SETS

**Materials:**
- *Coloured paper*
- *Varnish*
- *Scissors*
- *Strong glue*
- *Sticky tape*
- *Three or four boxes.*

*Suggested - one tall for pens and pencils, one very short for rubbers etc., one tall and thin for rulers, one short for paper fasteners. NB -you can use milk cartons cut to different sizes.*

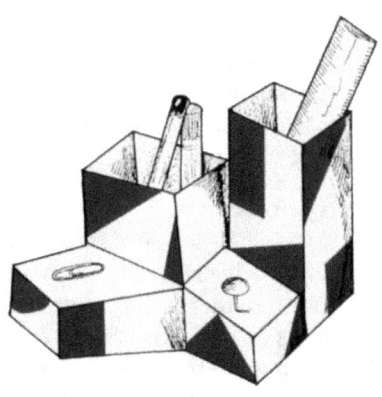

**Instructions:**
1. Glue the boxes together in the arrangement you want. Put the taller ones at the back so you can easily see into the shorter ones.
2. Cut the coloured paper into lots of small shapes
3. Paste the shapes onto the boxes so they cover the entire surface of all the boxes.
4. When this is dry, varnish with two to three coats of varnish

**Variations:**
- Instead of using shapes - cover the boxes with coloured paper or wrapping paper before sticking them together, or cover them with coloured paper and then stick magazine pictures on top.
- Try making each box look different.

# PLANT POTS

**Materials:**
- *One margarine tub*
- *Paint*
- *Varnish*

**Instructions:**
1. Wash and dry margarine tub thoroughly.
2. Paint your design thickly on the outside.
3. When paint is dry, apply two to three coats of varnish.

**Variations:**
- Cut some coloured paper into lots of shapes and paste them onto the tub, completely covering it.
- Cover with wrapping paper
- Cut out pictures from magazines to cover your tubs with.

# NOTEPAD HOLDER

**Materials:**
- Strong glue
- Icy pole sticks
- Cheap note pad
- Varnish

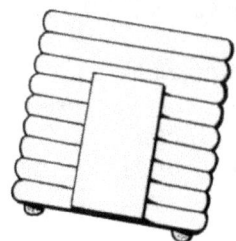

**Instructions:**
1. Arrange three icy pole sticks as per figure 1. Glue firmly.
2. Using very strong glue line up other sticks (figure 2) until the bottom two sticks are covered - making a flat board.
3. Attach the note pad to the flat board with some sticky tape.

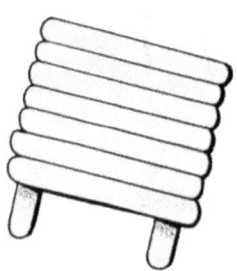

# PAPER AND CARD CRAFT

Place Mats
Woven Place Mats
Alphabet Picture Wall Frieze
Misfits Book

# PLACE MATS

**Materials:**
- *Strong white card*
- *Paint, textas or pencils*
- *Clear self-adhesive book covering*

**Instructions:**
1. Using scissors cut the cardboard to the size you would like; e.g. 30 cm x 25 cm.
2. Now, paint or draw on the cardboard an attractive, bright picture.
3. When the picture is dry, cover the back of the card with a piece of clear self-adhesive book covering which is 1 cm smaller all around than the placemat.
4. Now cover the front with a piece of book covering bigger than the mat. This will overlap to the back.

**Variations:**
- Why not have a picture on each side and have a reversible mat?
- Try cutting out and pasting shapes on instead of drawing a picture.
- Try cutting pictures from magazines to paste on.
- Why not name the mats for presents for your friends?

# WOVEN PLACE MATS

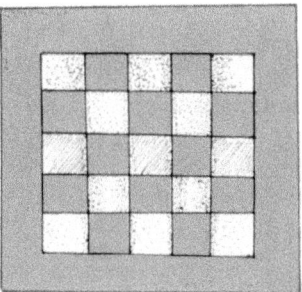

**Materials:**
- Several sheets of coloured paper or card in assorted colours.
- Scissors
- Ruler
- Pencil
- Paste
- Firm piece of cardboard

**Instructions:**
1. Take one sheet of coloured paper and cut it to 25 cm x 25 cm in size.
2. Fold this piece of paper in half so that the colour is on the inside.
3. Now, using the pencil and ruler draw parallel lines about 2 cm apart, leaving 2 cm at the open ends.

Example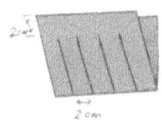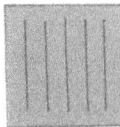

4. Cut along each line you have drawn making sure you stop 2 cm before the end.
5. Using the other colours (3 will do), cut each piece into strips 2 cm wide. These strips will form the weaving material.
6. Weave each strip through over and under, alternating colours or forming patterns. Make sure each piece fits snugly against the strip before it.
7. Using the paste, paste each end of the woven strips down.
8. Paste the mat onto a piece of firm cardboard the same size (i.e. 25cm x 25cm.
9. When dry either spray the mat with two to three coats of varnish or cover it with clear self-adhesive book covering.

# ALPHABET PICTURE WALL FRIEZE

**Materials:**

**Instructions:**
- *Twenty six pieces of card the same size, e.g. 17cm x 20cm*
- *Textas or crayons*
- *Magazines*
- *Paste*
- *Hole punch*
- *String*
- *Varnish*

**Instructions:**
1. Take the first card and write on it in big letters A or Aa.
2. Using the magazines cut out pictures of things starting with 'a' to paste onto the page.
3. Repeat steps 1 and 2 on the rest of the cards with the appropriate letter and pictures.
4. When the paste is dry spray the cards with two to three coats of varnish.
5. Punch the holes and string the cards together ready to hang on a wall.

**Variations:**
- Draw pictures of things starting with the appropriate letter
- Make a theme frieze, i.e. farms, families.

These make good presents for a young child's room.

# MISFITS BOOK

**Materials:**
- *Two pieces of card*
- *Various sheets of the same sized paper*
- *Magazines*
- *Scissors*
- *Paste*

**Instructions:**
1. Find an assortment of 'people' pictures the same size from the magazines.
2. Paste each picture on a piece of paper in the same position on each page.
3. When dry put the pages together and cut them into three pieces. Turning over different pieces creates different pictures.
4. Now decorate the front cover (one piece of card) as you wish and join your book together.
5. Join the front and back cover and other pages together with either string or staples. If using string punch holes down the left hand side with a hole punch and weave the string through - down to the bottom and back up to the top. Tie to secure.

**Variations:**
- Try drawing a picture for each page instead of using magazine pictures.
- Make a book using pictures of buildings, animals or other similar objects.

# OBTAINING MATERIALS

Varnish        Strong glue
Fabric         Colouring rice and macaroni
Card           Odds and Ends
Wadding        Collecting Pictures
Clay           Home made paste
Paints         Coloured Paper
Paper

## VARNISH

The varnish used in the activities in this book is designed to provide protection for the articles made. Spray varnish tends to be a lot easier to use than brush on varnish and both types are available from local hardware shops.

Two types of finish are also available. One is a satin or glossy finish and the other is a natural or matt finish. Whichever one you use will depend on your personal preference on type of finish.

## FABRIC

If you don't wish to buy fabric for small activities you can always use scrap fabric from someone you may know who sews or you could use old clothes (ask Mum first) that may be thrown away.

## CARD

For light types of card, food boxes are fine - i.e. cereal boxes, washing powder boxes etc.

For heavy card try some fruit or packaging boxes. Different card types are also available from newsagents and craft shops.

## WADDING

Wadding is a type of material used for stuffing cushions, soft toys, etc. It is available off the roll from fabric stores and craft shops.

## CLAY

There is now a type of clay available that doesn't require firing. It is available from most craft stores and school suppliers. If this is unavailable in your area try contracting your local school to find out where you can get your clay work fired.

## STRONG GLUE

There are many types of strong glues available. They can be bought from department stores, craft and hobby shops and school suppliers.

Suitable types for use are P.V.A. type glues, craft and hobby glues. "Super glue" should not be used by young children.

## COLOURING RICE, MACARONI, ETC.

Rice, macaroni, sand and all sorts of bits and pieces can be coloured by the use of food dye or edicol dyes.

Edicol dyes - mix a little edicol dye and water in a bowl and add uncooked rice, pasta, sand, etc. Wait until the objects have absorbed the colour. Strain the objects and dry on a newspaper or fly wire screen in the sun (or in a low oven turning frequently).

Edicol dyes are available from craft shops and school suppliers.

Food Colouring - use in the same manner as the edicol dyes. These are perhaps more readily available as you can purchase them from most supermarkets.

## COLLECTING ODDS AND ENDS

For bits and pieces that can be used in most craft activities, ask your friends and family to collect things, or look out for different types of things yourself.

Recycling depots are also useful for getting materials. These are places that collect different types of waste materials from other factories. To find your closest recycling depot look in the yellow pages phone book or contact your local school or kindergarten.

## COLLECTING PICTURES

As well as looking through magazines for pictures you can collect small pictures from the endless supplies of 'junk mail' that come through your home letterbox.

You can also get different types of advertising pictures from your local supermarket, newsagent, video shop or ask at the local travel agent for some 'round the world' pictures.

## HOME MADE PASTE

Home made paste is easily made and its ingredients are usually readily available. This paste is not as strong as many commercial pastes but is adequate for pasting paper to paper or paper and fabric to card.

A simple recipe follows:

### Flour and Water Paste

- 1/2 cup plain flour ⎫
- 1/2 cup cold water ⎬ Blend to a paste
- Add 600 ml boiling water and stir rapidly as it thickens. *It will further thicken as it cools.*

This paste will not keep for long periods of time but is safe if swallowed. Ask an adult to help you as children should not use boiling water.

## PAINTS

Paints are readily available in both powder and liquid form from craft shops and even most toy shops or childrens' educational stores.

## COLOURED PAPER

Coloured paper is available at newsagents, craft shops and school suppliers. It is a good idea to save wrapping paper as this is good in activities where coloured paper is required. It doesn't necessarily have to be plain paper.

## PAPER

Where 'normal' paper is required you can use paper purchased from a newsagent or craft shop, but it is a lot cheaper to use butcher's paper (available from the local butcher) or computer paper. This is obtainable from local shops or businesses which have computers.

# INDEX

Alphabet Picture Wall Frieze..........62
Basic Plastic Shaker......................46
Bird Mobile....................................2
Card ............................................66
Cardboard Cone Christmas Trees....30
Cardboard Finger Puppets.............26
Cat Dress-Up ...............................13
Christmas Decorations..................29
Clay .............................................66
Clay Print Wrap ...........................41
Collecting Odds And Ends.............67
Collecting Pictures........................67
Coloured Paper.............................68
Colouring Rice, Macaroni..............67
Cork Mobile....................................4
Desk Sets .....................................56
Doctor Dress-Up ..........................14
Double-sided Puzzles....................51
Dough Decorations.......................35
Dressing Up..................................11
Drumsticks...................................45
Egg Cup Bells ..............................33
Fabric...........................................66
Fan Fold Wrap .............................40
Felt Animal Mobile ........................7
Felt Finger Puppets .....................25
Gift Wrapping Papers ...................27
Headpieces...................................17
Home Made Paste........................68
Indian Girl Headpiece ..................18
Lid Cymbals.................................47
Light Globe Shaker.......................45
Magic Strips.................................31
Make Your Own Jigsaws ..............50
Make Your Own Puzzles...............49
Materials for Puppet-Making..........24
Mellagerphone .............................47
Misfits Book.................................63

Mobiles...........................................1
Multi-sided Box Puzzle .................54
Musical Instruments .....................43
Notepad Holder ...........................58
Obtaining Materials ......................65
Other Ideas for Dressing Up .........16
Paints...........................................68
Paper............................................68
Paper And Card Craft...................59
Paper Plate Puppets .....................27
Pasta Wreaths ..............................32
Place Mats...................................60
Plant Pots.....................................57
Princess Headpiece ......................21
Puppets........................................23
Puzzles ........................................44
Rubber Glove Puppets .................28
Sandwich Board Dress-Up ............14
Shaker Fillings..............................46
Space Creature Dress-Up..............12
Spaceman Headpiece ...................19
Spider Headpiece .........................21
Spiral Mobile..................................3
String and Woodblock Print Wrap..38
Storage Boxes, Design-Your-Own ...54
Strong Glue ..................................67
Surprise Picture Wrap..................39
Swagman Headpiece ....................20
Tin Drum .....................................44
Toilet Roll Puppets .......................28
Toy Bags .....................................55
Useful Containers.........................53
Varnish.........................................66
Vegetable Print Wrap....................37
Various Hanging Decorations ........34
Wadding.......................................66
Witch Headpiece ..........................20
Woven Place Mats........................61

SOME MORE BOOKS IN OUR CHILDRENS' SERIES:

**The Parents' Time Off Series:**

- Kids' Magical Activities
- Kids' Gardening Activities
- Kids' Cooking Activities
- Kids' Hands-On Craft Activities
- Kids' Fun Craft Activities
- Kids' Creative Craft Activities
- Kids' Games Book 1
- Kids' Games Book 2
- Kids' Nature Activities
- Kids' Holiday Activities

**Classic Fairytales from Tolkien's Bookshelf:**

- Grimms' Fairytales - Illustrated
- The Red Fairy Book - Illustrated
- The Princess and the Goblin - Illustrated.
- The Story of King Arthur and his Knights - Illustrated

Find out more on our website!

www.leavesofgoldpress.com

# THE PARENTS' TIME OFF SERIES

# Princess Pam Fell Into the Jam

More than a hilarious rhyme, this is a slapstick comedy that causes a riot of laughter when read aloud. Princess Pam and her messy sisters appeal to every child.

The rollicking rhymes, the unconventional story and the lively, detailed pictures combine to make one of the funniest and most original children's books published.

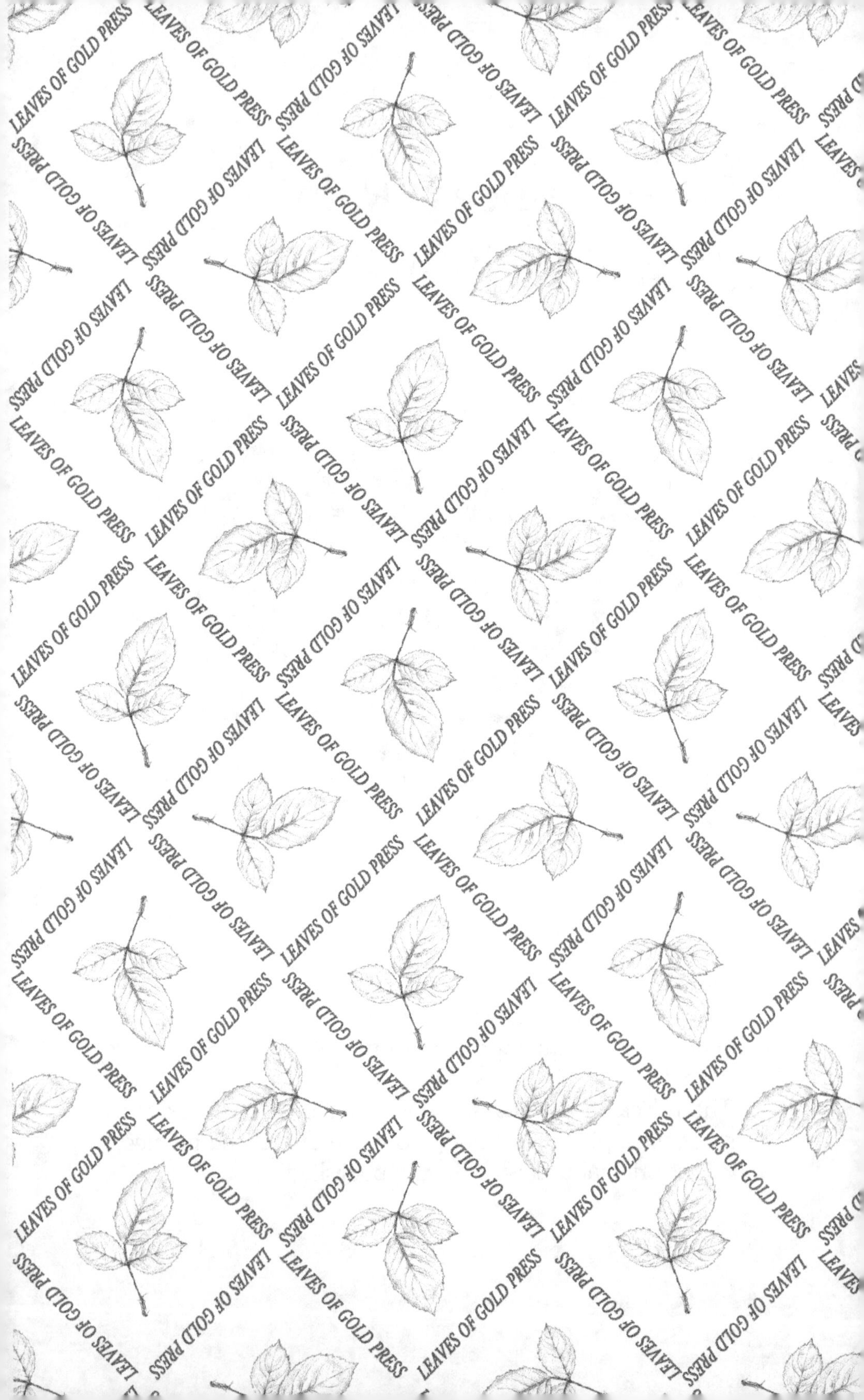
LEAVES OF GOLD PRESS

www.ingramcontent.com/pod-product-compliance
Lightning Source LLC
LaVergne TN
LVHW052256070426
835507LV00035B/3040